UNIVERSITY OF NORTH CAROLINA
STUDIES IN THE ROMANCE LANGUAGES AND LITERATURES

URBAN TIGNER HOLMES, JR., *Editor*

NICHOLSON B. ADAMS   JOHN CORIDON LYONS
ALFRED G. ENGSTROM   KARL-LUDWIG SELIG
ROBERT W. LINKER   STERLING A. STOUDEMIRE

JOHN ESTEN KELLER, *Managing Editor*

UNIVERSITY OF NORTH CAROLINA
STUDIES IN THE ROMANCE LANGUAGES AND LITERATURES
Number 36

FORMULAIC DICTION AND THEMATIC
COMPOSITION IN THE *CHANSON DE ROLAND*

FORMULAIC DICTION AND THEMATIC COMPOSITION IN THE *CHANSON DE ROLAND*

BY

STEPHEN G. NICHOLS, JR.

CHAPEL HILL

THE UNIVERSITY OF NORTH CAROLINA PRESS

Copyright, 1961, by
The University of North Carolina Press

Depósito Legal: V. 1 055 – 1961

PREFACE

The purpose of this paper is descriptive rather than definitive. It is an attempt to come to grips with certain undeniable textual characteristics, which are frequently ignored, in order to provide a better understanding of the basic textual conventions of the *Chanson de Roland*. In this fashion, it is hoped that the examination of these conventions will be able to contribute to a critical appreciation of this epic, and thus to broaden the ever-increasing foundation for the judgment that the *Chanson de Roland* is the masterpiece of its genre.

I would like to express my gratitude to Professor Lowry Nelson, Jr., and to Professor Adam Parry both of whom read the first manuscript of my study and made valuable suggestions for its improvement.

I am especially grateful for the support of Professor Konstantin Reichardt and Dean Hartley Simpson of Yale, who secured a grant-in-aid from the University toward the publication of this paper.

S. G. N., Jr.

New Haven, Connecticut
November 1960

The most expressive term that has emerged from the recent studies on oral poetry appeared in the French review *La Table Ronde,* which devoted its December 1958 issue to *l'épopée vivante.* The object of this issue was to confront the primary epics which were formerly "living" with those which are, in a few isolated places, still living today. The adjective *vivante* is particularly expressive of the nature of the primary epic, because of its connotation of action, of movement which suggests the way an oral tradition exists and is propagated in its environment. For the existence and propagation of an oral tradition, as the now classic studies of Milman Parry and Albert B. Lord[1] have shown, depend on conditions of composition and recitation which are quite distinct from those found in a literary tradition. In the present paper, I shall examine the Old French epic, the *Chanson de Roland,* from the point of view of formula, enjambement, and thematic composition, in order to demonstrate the textual characteristics which argue its oral rather than literary character.[2] The important textual characteristics to be

---

[1] For a bibliography of the writings of Milman Parry see Albert B. Lord, "Homer, Parry, and Huso", *AJA,* LII (1948), 34-44. (A collected edition of Milman Parry's writings is now being prepared by Adam Parry.) Mr. Lord's recent book, *The Singer of Tales* (Harvard, May 1960) appeared too late for me to use it in preparing this study.

[2] I shall not attempt in this paper to claim that the *Chanson de Roland* is a "dictated text" and was written down as it was sung. Not one piece of direct evidence could be advanced to support such an assertion. Furthermore, it seems much more likely that the poem was written down by someone trained in the oral tradition who may have used the relative leisure of a written endeavor to order the elements in the poem. My main concern is to demonstrate the clearly oral characteristics of the poem and to show how these do not preclude a critical analysis and evaluation, as F. M. Combellack seemed to feel in his article "Milman Parry and the Homeric Artistry", *Comparative Literature,* XI (summer 1959), 193-208. This article and Professor H. T. Wade-Gery's book, *The Poet of the Iliad* (Cambridge, 1952), appear to be based on the assumption that by proving that a poem belongs

considered are the composition of the decasyllabic line, the relation of the lines to each other (how they are connected), and the relation of the lines to the larger unit of narrative composition, the *laisse*. Once these first two phases of the study have considered the characteristics of the lines within the *laisse*, it will be necessary to examine the relation of the *laisses* to each other, in other words, the story motifs or themes which contribute to the totality of the narrative. Hence the third phase of the examination of oral characteristics will concentrate on the composition by theme in the *Chanson de Roland*. Once the initial study has demonstrated the traditional elements of this epic, I shall attempt to demonstrate how the usual methods of literary criticism can be adjusted so that a critical evaluation of the poem can be achieved, much as one can analyze a renaissance love sonnet in spite of its highly conventionalized form and content.

Milman Parry based his theories of the formula in Homeric verse on the need for the poet to fill a specified amount of verse in a way that would exactly fit the rhythmic needs of the verse. Thus, the hexametric verse was the controlling factor in the development of the Homeric formula. Within the single line, the formulas tended to conform in length to the breaks in the line made by the caesurae. Since there is no other poetic unit of construction in the Homeric verse besides the hexametric line, Parry had only that unit to consider in developing his theories. While the single line is still the basic unit of construction in the Old French epics, there is a larger unit which must be considered, the *laisse*. As indicated in the introduction, the linear action of the *Roland* moves from *laisse* to *laisse* with the individual lines within each *laisse* developing an idea which is frequently stated in the first line of the *laisse*. Thus the first *laisse* of *Roland* begins:

    Carles li reis, nostre emper[er]e magnes

and the rest of the *laisse* fills in the pertinent information concerning Charlemagne's activities at the moment when the epic opens. Thus

---

to an oral tradition, one automatically precludes any possibility of that work's reflecting "a creative genius".

each *laisse* has a unity of its own, expressed structurally by the assonance or homophony of the final tonic vowel in each line within the *laisse*. Ultimately, of course, the poet's task is to compose not only a series of individual *laisses* but to unify these according to the themes he wishes to express in the poem. Nevertheless, the immediate problem of the poet is the composition of the *laisse*, and, consequently, of the individual lines of which it consists. For, as Jean Rychner demonstrated in his recent work, *La Chanson de geste: essai sur l'art épique des jongleurs*,[3] the *laisse*, like the ballad stanza, existed as an aide to facilitate the singer's improvisation. Thus the singer could concentrate on composing the *laisse*, which could then be related periodically to the succeeding one. This provided him with a convenient, mentally conceivable unit in contrast to the expanse of the entire poem. Furthermore, the *chanson* was characterized by a tune which followed the *laisse* and which was probably repeated in each *laisse*.[4] The very flexibility in the length of the *laisse* attests that it served the poet's needs and was not a rigid literary-poetic form like the sonnet. In the *Chanson de Roland*, the *laisses* average fourteen lines with the shortest of five lines (XXVI, LX), and the longest of thirty-four (LIV) and thirty-five lines (CCXXVII). In only three cases does one *laisse* overflow into another (XXII-XXIII, XLIV-XLV, LX-LXI) and these are the result of speeches which, judging from the manuscript variations, and the brevity of the following *laisses* in each case, seem to have been separated either because of some confusion on the part of the scribes, or in order to emphasize the climactic points in the speeches. Aside from the three exceptions already mentioned, as Jenkins observes in his edition:

> The end of the *laisse* is ... strongly marked by the final line, which is usually independent in syntax, and summary, sententious, or climactic in content. The final line was probably further indicated by a crescendo or forte in the music. [as one theory on the direction *AOI* at the end of the *laisse* finds].[5]

---

[3] Jean Rychner, *La Chanson de geste: essai sur l'art épique des jongleurs* (Genève, 1955).
[4] *Ibid*. pp. 18-19.
[5] *La Chanson de Roland*, Oxford Version, ed. T. A. Jenkins, rev. ed. (Boston, 1924), p. cxliv.

Thus, the *laisse* is certainly the main unit of construction in the Old French *chansons de geste*, but one must not forget the unit of construction of the *laisse*, the individual, decasyllabic line.[6] In the Old French epic line, as in the decasyllabic line of Southslavic heroic poetry, the caesura falls after the fourth syllable. This means that the expression in the first four syllables (hereafter called the A-verse)[7] would have to be relatively short, while the final six syllables (hereafter called the B-verse) could contain a slightly longer expression. In its simplest form, this means that there would be a subject in the A-verse and an object in the B-verse which would relate what the subject did. Of course, this is an oversimplification for not every line has the subject in the A-verse and the object in the B-verse, but the causal factor for such a division, the caesura, is always present, requiring that the line be filled by two co-ordinate elements.

The inter-relation of the two parts of the decasyllabic epic line is much more easily demonstrated than discussed abstractly, however, so let us examine the lines from the following *laisse*, chosen at random, to see how the lines themselves are composed, how they are connected, and how they develop the subject of the *laisse* (indicated in the first line). Following Lord[8] and Magoun,[9] I have underlined with a solid line those phrases which belong to a formulaic system (bcause they appear elsewhere in the same metrical circumstances to express the same idea), and have underlined with a broken line those phrases which, syntactically and rhythmically,

---

[6] The basic hierarchy in the units of construction has been quite ignored in Rychner's book, cited above, with the result that he has overlooked the nature and the extent of the formulaic system which underlies the *Chanson de Roland*, contenting himself only with whole-line formulas in the battle descriptions, thus ignoring the method of construction of the rest of the poem.

[7] By "A-verse" I mean the tetrasyllabic hemistich of the French decasyllabic, epic line. Similarly, I use "B-verse" for the hexasyllabic hemistich. In using "A-verse" and "B-verse" for the Old French decasyllabic hemistiches, I do not mean to imply that these are complete verse units as is the Anglo-Saxon "A-verse" or "B-verse". I use the terms rather for convenience, to avoid long and awkward repetitions.

[8] A. B. Lord, *Four Symposia on Folklore*, ed. Stith Thompson (Bloomington, Indiana, 1953), p. 308.

[9] F. P. Magoun, Jr., "Oral-Formulaic Character of Anglo-Saxon Poetry", *Speculum*, XXVIII (1953), p. 449.

appear similar to other formulas, but which do not appear elsewhere in the work analyzed.[10]

IV

> Dist Blancandrins: "Pa[r] ceste meie destre
> E par la barbe ki al piz me ventelet,
> L'ost des Franceis verrez sempres desfere.
> Francs s'en irunt en France, la lur tere.
> Quant cascuns ert a sun meillor repaire,
> Carles serat ad Ais, a sa capele;
> A seint Michel tendrat mult halte feste.
> Vendrat li jurz, si passerat li termes,
> N'orrat de nos paroles ne nuveles.
> Li reis est fiers e sis curages pesmes:
> De noz ostages ferat tre[n]cher les testes;
> Asez est mielz qu'il i perdent les testes;
> Que nus perduns clere Espaigne, la bele
> Ne nus aiuns les mals ne les suffraites."
> Dient paien: "Issi poet il ben estre."
>
> (lines 47-61)[11]

The *laisse* is clearly an expansion of the first two words, *Dist Blancandrins*, since every line except the last is devoted to the speech indicated in the first line. The final line is a common collective response which indicates that the speech and the *laisse* are concluded. It also reflects the reaction of the rhetorical audience within the story. Parenthetically, such final lines remind the listener that the story is supposed to include plurality of personages, although, in actual fact, only the central figures ever act or speak.

There is a clear distinction between the A-verse of the first line of the *laisse* and the B-verse, since the A-verse is a "discourse introduction" formula, and the B-verse is the beginning of the

---

[10] Needless to say, I use Parry's definition of the formula as, "a group of words which is regularly employed under the same metrical conditions to express a given, essential idea". (*Harvard Studies in Classical Philology*, XLI (1930), p. 80.) Professor Magoun (*op. cit.*), for the purpose of his analysis of Anglo-Saxon poetry, showed that, in shorter metrical units than the Homeric hexameter, it was also possible for a single word, as well as a group of words, to comply with Parry's definition.

[11] All line references will be to *Les Textes de la Chanson de Roland*, édités par Raoul Mortier, I (La Version d'Oxford), Paris, 1940.

discourse. This particular A-verse, "discourse introduction" formula, *Dist Blancandrins*, occurs six times in the first 500 lines of the poem, but the formulaic system itself (*dist* and a name/title/noun of three syllables in the nominative case) occurs forty times in the first 2000 lines of the poem, although it is just one type of "discourse introduction" formula. The B-verse of the first line is a "swearing formula" in which the speaker swears by his beard, by a saint, or in this case by his right hand. Ordinarily, the "swearing formula" is found in the A-verse so that the oath sworn may follow in the B-verse. The reason that the beard is frequently the thing sworn by in the A-verse (five times) is perhaps because the feminine hypersyllable [*E par la barb(e), Par ceste barb(e)*] is tolerated before the caesura, and in fact occurs two or three times in every *laisse* (as in lines 2 and 11 in this *laisse*), so that such a construction could invariably be used without having to be adjusted to the assonant requirements which affect B-verse formulas.[12] Notice that in the B-verse of this first line, the *jongleur* has substituted the two syllable *meie* for the *la* which one might expect (by comparison with *barbe*), in order to adjust the formula to the hypersyllabic pattern of the B-verses in this *laisse*, where, because of the feminie assonance, all the B-verses have an extra syllable. The same process was necessary in line 1719 where, however, the more frequent *barbe* has been used instead of *destre*:

Dist Oliver: "Par ceste meie barbe.

Although in this latter case the poet continues with the speech in the following line, in the *laisse* under consideration he ornaments the speech by adding another line where the A-verse swearing

---

[12] But note that in the later *chanson de geste* of the cycle of Guillaume d'Orange, *Le Charroi de Nimes*, the swearing formulas in the A-verse are more regular, having, in two out of three types, four syllables:

(4 plus 1)	*Par cel apostre*	(ll. 405, 513, 617)
(4)	*Par saint Denis*	(ll. 740, 1308)
(4)	*Par Mahomet*	(ll. 1227, 1261, 1382, 1450).

The same is true of the swearing formulas in *Le Couronnement de Louis*:

(4)	*Par saint Denis*	(ll. 547, 1260, 1641, 1756)
(4)	*Par Mahomet*	(ll. 874, 922, 962).

formula is followed by a B-verse expansion which really has nothing to do with what will eventually be said. The B-verse of this second line is, nevertheless, a very good example of how the line division into two parts does not have to be used to express subject-object, but may be used as an expansion or qualification of the subject, as the relative clause *ki al piz me ventelet* is here used. The same usage occurs in line 1107, although in that line the poet has substituted *cuardet* for the *ventelet* in our example, in answer to the different assonance of *laisse* LXXXVII. Note, however, that both words are tri-syllabic so the substitution has no effect on the formula length. The A-verse of line 3 in *laisse* IV has been marked with a broken line because, although it fits a prevalent formulaic system, there is no other occurance of this particular phrase in *Roland*. The system to which it clearly belongs in the "article *plus* noun *plus* de (des) *plus* noun" (A-verse) of which their are thirteen other examples in the *Chanson de Roland* alone.[13] In purpose (second noun qualifying the first), we see that this system is similar to the "noun *plus* descriptive adjective" (A-verse) system of which the A-verse of line 11 in this *laisse* is an example. In the system exemplified by line 3, the qualification depends on the genetival use of the noun *Franceis,* but the effect is the same as the possessive qualification in line 11, *de noz hostages*. The A-verse of line 11 is further parallel to line 3 since it, too, is in the accusative case. Notice that, although the B-verses of both lines 3 and 11 are non-formulaic, in both cases there is an inversion in which in line 3 the object of the main verb, and in line 11 the prepositional phrase modifying *testes,* are placed in the A-verse, while the main verbs (subjects understood from the inflection) are placed at the beginning of the B-verse. Such an inversion would seem more complicated than saying the line in a natural, conversational order such as "you will soon see the French army undone", or, "he will have the heads of our hostages cut off", yet, as we have seen, the A-verses belong to formulaic systems in which noun preposition *plus* possessive

---

[13] *La gent de France* (590), *l'anme de lui* (1553, 3647), *l'amne del cors* (2940), *l'anme del conte* (2396), etc. The same system is found in other *chansons de geste* with the same formulas; cf. for example, *la flor de France* (Roland 2455, Charroi 686); *al brant d'acier* (Roland 3791, Couronnement de Louis* 2158).

pronoun adjective *plus* noun (in either the nominative or accusative) very frequently appear. When the accusative is used in such a manner, it invariably means an inversion because (as shall be seen later) there is little necessary enjambement in this poem, of the sort which would place a subject in the B-verse of a preceding line and its object in the A-verse of the following line. It must be supposed, then, that the *jongleur* found such an inversion as demonstrated by lines 3 and 11 easier, because of the formulaic nature of the A-verse, than saying the verse in a periodic sequence, i.e. subject-object.

Apropos of what Parry said concerning the refining action of tradition which gradually makes each formula the most poetic way of expressing an idea, notice that in both lines 3 and 11 the effect of the inversion is to place the two most important elements of the idea expressed at the points of heaviest stress, the fourth and tenth syllables. Thus *Franceis-desfere* in line 3, and *ostages-testes* in line 11 fall on the final syllables of the A- and B-verses. Such examples illustrate strikingly that formulas do not have a merely mechanical existence, they also contribute to the artistic ends of the tradition making the language a *Kunstsprache* in the fullest sense of the word.

The A-verse of the fourth line belongs to the same general formulaic system as the A-verse of the final line of the *laisse*. This is the "collective noun (plural, nominative) *plus* verb" (A-verse). (The final line, of course, is specifically a "discourse introduction" formula.) Altogether there are some thirty examples of this type of formula in the first 2000 lines of the poem. The B-verse of line 4 represents the type of formula which allows the poet to state a place name in the B-verse and to fill out the rest of the verse with an adjective or, as here, an adjective and a noun which is really redundant since *la lor tere* repeats the essential idea expressed by *en France*. Sometimes the preposition *plus* adjective *plus* place name will be found in syllables 6/7-10 while the first two/three syllables of the B-verse are used for a verb. An example of such a formula would be the B-verse of line 458, *ki seit en cest païs*. The formula in line 4 of our *laisse*, however, is quite frequent (as the basic similarity of the B-verse of line 6 indicates) being repeated exactly in line 808, and with the substitution of *nostre* for *la lor* in line 804.

With the A-verse of line 5, a new sentence begins. Notice that this sentence of five lines repeats in its first two lines (lines 5 and 6) the essence of what has already been said in lines 3 and 4. In the case of lines 3 and 4, the idea of the departure of the French for France was merely stated. In this second sentence, it will not only be stated, but also expanded to include the idea "that once the French are out of Spain, they will be too far away to know what we are doing". On this small scale, we see that the progression of ideas through the *laisse* is frequently a sort of hesitation step in which sentences are related one to the other by a repetition of the last idea in the preceding sentence, with further development of this idea in the following sentence. This observation is important, since we shall eventually see that the *laisses* are frequently related in the same way. The A-verse of line 5, in which the first word is *Quant,* indicates that the sentence will be organized on the syntactical pattern: "when... then". The A-verse of line 5 belongs to the general formulaic group, "preposition/conjunction/ adjective *plus* noun/pronoun and/or verb". The *quant* branch of this system is quite frequent, twenty-four times, and this particular formula, *Quant iert...* appears five times in the first 2000 lines, although this is the only case where the pronoun appears between *quant* and *iert*. Parry would undoubtedly see in such a deviation a clear case of scribal error, but such an assertion would argue an infallibility of the formula impossible to prove. *Repaire* in the B-verse of line 5 appears in line 661 where it is the final word in the line, but does not have *meillor* between the possessive adjective and itself. The infinitive form of the verb *repairer,* and various other forms of the verb occur in the same, final position in lines 36, 289, and 1969. These five uses of the two forms of the same word in the same place in the line certainly warrant its being considered as fulfilling a metrical need of the poet, and therefore of being formulaic (since the essential idea of dwelling is always expressed).

Carles serat, the A-verse of line 6 is a frequent formula of the type "name/title/pronoun *plus* être" (A-verse). There are twenty-seven examples of this formulaic system, though there are 372 examples of the general system "name/noun *plus* verb" (A-verse) to which this particular formula belongs. Since Charlemagne is the main figure in the poem, with whom the epic begins and ends, one could argue that the two syllable *Carles,* as it invariably appears in the nominative case as the first word in the A-verse, might be a formula itself. *Ad Ais a sa capele* in the B-verse is a type of formula already discussed in connection with the B-verse of line 4. In one use of this formula, *Ad Ais* has been switched from the fifth and sixth syllable position which is found also in line 478, to the ninth and tenth syllable position to fit the assonance of *laisse* LVII. *A seint Michel* in the A-verse of line 7 is an example of the type of inversion discussed above in connection with lines 3 and 11. Here the prepositional phrase, used adverbially to modify the main verb *tendrat* which holds the relatively weak fifth/sixth syllable position in the B-verse, is placed first with the result that the ideas of the place and the feast receive the stress. In lines 1427 and 2394 one also finds this formula with a substitution of the prepositions *de* and *e*, but no alteration of meaning or position. The B-verse of the ninth line does not seem to be separated from the *de nos* of the third and fourth syllables of the A-verse. Actually, *nos* is not the possessive pronoun plural of *notre*, but the pronoun *nous*. It is the omission of *ni* before *paroles* (a frequent omission in Old French) which seems to make the two parts of the line run together. The B-verse is a very common type of formulaic expression where two nouns or adjectives almost identical in meaning are used to fill the B-verse and are connected by *ni* or *e*: for example, *e prozdom e vaillant* (1. 1636); *traisun e murdrie* (1. 1475); *e la bronie e le cors* (1586). A frequent variant of this formula is the filling of the B-verse with two names, *Rollant e Oliver*, for instance. Altogether these two aspects of the formula occur thirty-three times up to line 2000.

Li reis est fiers in line 10 demonstrates the versatility which can be achieved by combining formulas. *Li reis* in the first two syllables of the A-verse appears eighteen times before line 1500, and is part of the larger formulaic system where a title in the nominative such as *li quens, li ber* appears in the first two syllables of the A-verse followed either by a proper name in two syllables or a verb. This formulaic expression occurs twenty-eight times before line 2000. Similar to this is the formulaic system in which the name is found in the first two syllables with the title following. Here in line 10, the formula "title/name *plus* verb" is combined with the formulaic system "title/name/noun *plus* descriptive adjective". Such a combination occurs also in such A-verses as *Rollant est proz* and *battaille est grante*. In the B-verse, *e sis corages pesmes* is of the formulaic types in which the B-verse further modifies or describes the subject of the A-verse. *Mult pesmes e fiers, e ledes les orilles* are two of the sixty-five examples of this formulaic system in the first 2000 lines. Line 11 has already been dscussed, but notice that lines 10 and 11, despite the fact that *li reis.* (1. 10) is the explicit subject of *ferat* (1. 11), are connected only paratactically. (Mortier emphasizes their relation by putting a colon after line 10; Jenkins uses no punctuation.) As we have seen in lines 3, 7, and 9, the subject of the main verb is frequently understood from the inflected form of the verb and therefore not explicit, but here (although lines 10 and 11 are independent statements with no necessary enjambement connecting them) there is yet a closer relationship —an unperiodic enjambement (of which more later)— between the two lines than between lines 6 and 7, for example, where there is no unperiodic enjambement.

Asez est mielz is found in the same position and with the same meaning in line 43 (Blancandrin's first speech) where the sense of the line is the same as in line 58 (line 12 of our *laisse*). One would perhaps tend to attribute the reduplication to the proximity of the two lines and say this is merely repetition and not formulaic. Nevertheless, the B-verses of both lines which say essentially the same thing are different to a degree which can not be caused simply by the different assonance of the two *laisses*. If one looks at the lines immediately following in either case, he will find exactly the same situation with the A-verses *Que nos perduns* identical while the B-verses differ. Actually, this is characteristic of what seem to be whole-line repetitions in *Roland*: the A-verses will be identical, while the B-verses differ. Such is the case, for instance, in lines 526, 541, 554 where the A-verse *Tanz colps ad pris* is followed by three entirely different, but clearly identifiable B-verse formulas. Such examples illustrate the versatility with which formulas may be combined and re-combined. These examples are also interesting from the psychological point of view, as we can see that the first elements of lines, being shorter and more prominent, were more apt to be used without modification, while the B-verse situation resulting from the proposition of the A-verse could be resolved with greater variety.

Line 14 is particularly interesting because of the syntactic connection of the two parts by *ne...ne*. Line 9, here, had the same construction, but the definite article was missing before the first noun in the B-verse. The two nouns which fill the B-verse are of the same formulaic system discussed in connection with line 9. Likewise, the final line has already been considered in the remarks on the characteristic structure of this *laisse*.

The rather lengthy analysis of the formulas in *laisse* IV was necessary to demonstrate the role of the formulas within the single lines of the *laisse,* and the relation of the formulas to the formulaic systems. Before going on to discuss the second oral-poetic characteristic of the *Roland,* the enjambement, the reader's attention is directed to *Appendix I* where the formula types and their prevalence in the first 2000 lines of the poem are listed. On this evidence, based for convenience sake on A-verse formulas only, it may be stated that the A-verses in 1157 of the first 2000 lines of the poem are formulaic. This means that over fifty percent, or one out of every two lines begins with a formula. Such a finding is consistent with the *laisse* analyzed above, although there a somewhat higher percentage of the A-verses was found to be formulaic.

In the analysis of *laisse* IV, we observed that the decasyllabic line was usually the unit of thought at the basic level, though the *laisse* itself expresses one or several ideas which advance the narrative. We are now concerned, however, with the basic level, the decasyllabic line. For the research on oral-poetic chararteristics has shown that oral poetry is characterized by non-enjambement, or unperiodic enjambement, while literate epic poetry where there is no need for the thought to be completed in a specific metrical unit, shows more of a tendency to carry the periods over several lines. Thus a line may end with a subject whose object may be in the next line, or even, if the next line is an ornamentation of the subject, in the line after that. There is thus a very much higher percentage of "necessary (periodic) enjambement" in literate poetry.[14]

---

[14] Milman Parry first published his findings concerning the importance of enjambement in distinguishing between oral and written styles in his article, "The Distinctive Character of Enjambement in Homeric Verse", *TAPA,* 60 (1929), pp. 200-220. He defined the aim of his study thus: "to seize more surely the way in which the thought of the poet unfolds from verse to verse...". (P. 203.) To achieve his goal, he defined "three ways in which the sense at the end of one verse can stand in relation to the sense at the beginning of the next: (1) the statement in the verse may be complete at the end of the verse. The next line will then be a new statement. In such

Parry and Lord who have published the largest amount of material on this particular subject have demonstrated that while oral narrative poetry has a particularly low incidence of necessary enjambement, and a correspondingly high incidence of end-stopped lines which contain in themselves a complete thought, it is the unnecessary enjambement which is especially important to the composition of oral narrative. For unperiodic enjambement permits the poet to join his formulas in free association enabling him to expand his matter paratactically as his mind ranges.

It is not the place here, however, to make a close stylistic exploration of the different uses of enjambement in the *Chanson de Roland*, but rather to show that this stylistic trait does exist in strikingly similar degree to that found by Lord in his analysis of the Southslavic decasyllabic epic verse,[15] and to demonstrate briefly how this oral characteristic is closely related to the use of the formulas already examined. For this purpose let us first examine an example of unnecessary enjambement to see how the poet may add free ideas to thoughts already essentially complete by the addition of new word groups. *Laisse* XIII offers a typical example of the use of unnecessary enjambement for a descriptive elaboration which translates an intangible desire, the desire of Marsile for Charlemagne to quit Spain, into materialistic terms of great splendor. The first two lines of the laisse are complete in themselves, that is they do not run over to the following lines for completion of the thought expressed in them. Line 180 is a "discourse introduction" formula in which the audience to be addressed is cited in the vocative in the A-verse, while the person speaking is identified in the B-verse. The following line is the beginning of Charlemagne's speech where he states the matter to be considered: the message

---

a case there is no enjambement. (2) the line end may coincide with the end of a word group so that the sentence at the end of the line gives a complete thought. But the period may continue to the next line, adding free ideas by new word groups. This is *unperiodic enjambement* [i.e. syntactically unnecessary]. (3) the verse end can fall at the end of a word group where there is not a complete thought, or it can fall in the middle of a word group; in both cases the enjambement is necessary to complete the thought and syntax of the period". (*Ibid.*, p. 203.)

[15] Lord extended Parry's research into the realm of Southslavic epic in his article, "Homer and Huso III: Enjambement in Greek and Southslavic Heroic Song", *TAPA* 79 (1948), pp. 113-24.

of Marsile. The next line touches upon the first part of the message. So far the three lines have been three complete ideas, all related to be sure, but related by juxtaposition. This steady progression from one idea to another is interrupted with line 183, however. Instead of the corollary to the idea in line 182 (i.e. the reason for Marsile's proffered gifts which actually comes in line 187), there is an expansion of the idea expressed by *aveir* and especially by *grant masse* in line 182. This expansion covers four lines where each line contains an explicit reference to one or two of the gifts. Again there is no close grammatical interconnection of the lines so that one or all could be omitted without affecting the sense of the passage. Yet while a line such as,

Li reis Marsilie m'ad tramis ses messages   (1. 181)

is recognizably a statement of fact being passed from speaker to audience (subject, object, indirect object), the catalogue of gifts is only explicable in the context by reference to the line which precedes it:

De sun aveir me voelt duner grant masse.   (1. 182)

The catalogue is thus a paratactic expansion of *grant masse*, although that idea is complete in its own line and does not *require* expansion. Nevertheless, the poet is able to develop the idea of *grant masse*, and the development is far from being a useless bit of padding. The catalogue of gifts has been repeated more briefly in *laisse* VII by the narrator, then more completely by Blancandrin in *laisse* IX (using the same formulas as here, and in the same order), and now is repeated by Charlemagne himself in *laisse* XIII. This repetition (always made possible by the opportunity offered by unnecessary enjambement to expand an idea from line to line without the limitation of a tight grammatical linking) serves a triple purpose. It makes Marsile's desire for Charlemagne to quit Spain emphatically tangible by the splendor of the wealth he is willing to pay to accomplish his purpose; it underlines the greatness of Charlemagne that he should be the object of such rich gifts; and finally, it provides a very concrete motive for the French to quit Spain honorably. This last purpose is also the basis for the first clash between Roland and Ganelon (*laisses* XIV and XV).

Although unnecessary enjambement gives the text the appearance of freedom of expansion so important to the ornamentation of the basic action (catalogues of the heroes, their descriptions, etc.), there is another method of joining the verses which is also important. This characteristic is the tendency for just over half of the lines analyzed to show no enjambement at all: to be related by juxtaposition of the successive ideas within the lines themselves. When speaking of the decasyllabic line as the basic unit of construction, it was noted that the formulas filled just that metric length (the decasyllable) or part of it. Thus the basic thoughts tend to be complete within a part or the whole of the decasyllable itself. For this reason the next line will rather be related to its predecessor by the relation of its content, its thought, to the content of the preceding line instead of by a complex sequence of subordinate clauses or other grammatical devices. Hence a period, if it extends over several lines, has the character of a series of main clauses. This method of joining the lines has the effect of a sequence of brief statements which can be extremely effective in imparting speed to dramatic narrative. Thus, for example, in *laisse* XXV where Charlemagne proffers the glove and baton to Ganelon, who drops them, thereby foreshadowing the coming disaster, the narrative proceeds in a series of single-line statements each conveying one aspect or action in the tense situation. There are only six lines, but in these six lines the contradictory forces which spark the tragedy flare for an instant, finally culminating in Ganelon's cryptic remark:

'Seigneurs', dist Guenes, 'vos en orrez noveles'!

We have seen how the two major stylistic means for joining verses in the *Chanson de Roland* are used. It may be possible to obtain some perspective of this usage by comparing the results of a quantitative analysis of two series of lines from the *Chanson de Roland* [See Appendix II] with examples from known, literate Old French poetry. For this purpose, I have examined two passages from *Le Chevalier de la Charrete* (octasyllabic) of Chrétien de Troyes, and one of the chansons of Thibaut IV de Navarre (decasyllabic). The results of these anlyses may be seen in Appendix II. From these findings, it is immediately apparent that while there is a comparable incidence of non-enjambement in the *Roland* and the lines from Chrétien de Troyes, there is almost a reversal of the amount of necessary and unnecessary enjambement in Chrétien as compared with the *Roland*. While only eight instances of necessary enjambement were recorded in the first 500 lines of the *Roland* (mostly of the construction 'when... then', cf. 11. 51-52), there are twenty-nine instances of necessary enjambement in the first series of sixty-five lines in Chrétien and thirty in the second series. (An example of necessary enjambement in Chrétien not found in the *Chanson de Roland* would be 11. 4654-55 of *Le Chevalier de la Charrete* (éd. de M. Roques, CFMA) where the direct object of the verb *estant, ses bras*, is found at the beginning of the line following that which holds the main verb.) Conversely there are only six examples of unnecessary enjambement in the first series of sixty-five lines from Chrétien, and four in the second series. On the other hand there are 231 instances of unnecessary enjambement in the first 500 lines of *Roland*.

These results, on a much smaller scale, are borne out by the *chanson* of Thibaut de Navarre which begins:

Mi grant desir e tuit mi grief torment.[16]

Here, in the forty-one lines of the *chanson*, one finds eighteen instances of necessary enjambement [see Appendix II], sixteen lines with no enjambement, and seven which have unnecessary enjambement. Lack of space prevents citing more examples of the striking difference in the use of enjambement in the known literary Old French poets and the *Chanson de Roland*, but the indications of the material which has been presented should at least suggest that there is a difference, and that the method of joining the lines in the *Chanson de Roland* is closely identified with the formulaic construction of the lines. In other words, where Chrétien de Troyes could end one thought in the middle of a line and begin a new one which carries over into the next line as in the following example:

---

[16] I use the text given in Bartsch's *Chrestomathie de l'ancien français* (12° éd., Leipzig, 1920), pp. 186-87.

Et cil respont qu'il i avoit
un cimetire; et cil li dist:
'Menez m'i, se Dex vos aïst;
(*Le Chevalier de la Charrete*, 11. 1852-54).

the *Chanson de Roland* would take one line for each thought:

Guenes respunt; 'Itels est sis curages;
Jamais n'ert hume ki encuntre lui vaille.'
(11. 375-76).

The preceding two sections have dealt with the predominance of the formula, and of the method of joining lines in the Oxford text of the *Chanson de Roland*. The first characteristic permits the poet's language to be as general as possible, so that the same or similar expressions and ways of saying things may be applied to the greatest range of situations possible. The second characteristic adjusts the extent of a basic thought to one line where the formula acts to make the thought fit that space by lengthening or compressing it so that there will be no occasion to start a new thought in the middle of a line which might have to run over into the next line to be completed. If one consideres the *Chanson de Roland* more generally, he will find that there are larger forces which reflect the textual characteristics already discussed. He will find that there is a very cogent reason why the formula can be used in different situations, and this quite simply is that the variety of situation is kept to a minimum by the themes around which the poem is composed. It was noted earlier that the discussion of theme would deal mostly with the larger unit of construction, the *laisse*. It will be necessary, though, to keep the formula in mind because this is the smallest verbal unit, the basis from which the ideas in the mind begin to be given audible expression. James A. Notopoulos has outlined the connection between idea and expression as follows:

> ...the technique of oral composition, which is generic in character, leaves its imprint on the mind of the oral poet and accounts in large measure for the growth of generic typology and mentality. Despite the separation caused by philosophical or literary analysis, there is in actuality a very deep and intimate association between the mind and the words. It is this very close relationship which constitutes

the basis of the belief that the generic in Homer originates with the technique of oral composition. Even as the artist can only express ideas for which he has techniques, so the verbal artist can only express ideas in proportion to the formulas that he acquires from tradition or adds to his tradition.[17]

In fact, in the next section, it will be shown that the outstanding oral poet can express ideas outside of his formulas, but for the present inquiry, this is an excellent statement of the relation between the thematic conception of ideas and their formulaic expression.

From the very first lines the generic and typological characteristics of the *Chanson de Roland* are manifest. The first *laisse* tells us that "our great emperor Charles has spent seven years in Spain which he has conquered from the sea to the highest mountain. Fortified castles, walled cities all have been breached and taken by him, except for Saragossa. Saragossa is held by King Marsile who serves Mohammed and Apollo". Charlemagne is quite obviously a type, or more properly an archetype who represents the ultimate in strong and wise leadership as well as the militant defender of the faith and patriarch of his people. As the poem goes on, his attributes become more and more archetypal. His great age, *plus ad de II. C. anz*, his hoary head and beard, *ki est canuz e vielz, ki est canuz e blancs*, are all stressed on different occasions. Moreover, as Zeus had Herakles in the war against the Titans, as Oðinn had Baldr, and as God had Christ, Cherlemagne has the youthful Roland to supplement his powers:

> Quant ier il mais d'osteier recreant?
> —Ço n'iert,' dist Guenes, 'tant cum vivet Rollant.
> (11. 543-44, 556-57)

Other elements in the first *laisse* contribute to the generalizing effect. Seven years as the length of time Charlemagne has been in Spain is a very general number, used quite frequently: *set cenz camelz* (11. 31, 129, 184, 645); *set anz* (1. 197); *.vii. milie graisles* (1.1454); and elsewhere. *All* cities and *all* castles fall before Charlemagne

---

[17] James A. Notopoulos, "Generic and Oral Composition in Homer", *TAPA*, LXXXI (1950), p. 34.

except the one which is the epitome of everything paganism stands for, Saragossa. This symbolism is important, for the story is not merely a history of treason and defeat, nor the story of a war between two kings, it is the battle of Christianity against paganism with Charles as the symbol of Christianity, while Baligant, the Emir of Cairo and thus the greatest pagan figure, represents the evils opposed to Christianity. These may be bald terms, but the defeat at Roncevaux does become a victory with the apotheosis of Roland and the defeat of the Saracen forces by Charlemagne. This is certainly not where the greatness of the *Chanson de Roland* lies as an heroic poem, but the generalizing tendencies of such identifications as Charlemagne with Christianity and the Saracen leaders with paganism certainly require some such allegorical consideration as indicated by the famous line:

Paien unt tort e chrestiens unt dreit. (1. 1015)

In this respect line 8 is certainly indicative of a Christian-Pagan polarity where the Greek god Apollo is included with Mohammed thus indicating the extent to which all non-Christian religions were combined. It is important to understand the polarity of the types good and bad, Christian and Pagan in the poetic conception of the characters because on these polarities much of the story turns. Formulaically, these polarities might be expressed *mult est bon* or *mult est fel*. They are seen in the treacherous plans laid in the first part of the poem; again in the battle themes of the second[18] and third parts; and finally in the trial and judgment of Ganelon (where, as in the third part, justice triumphs and the felon is published) in the fourth section. These themes may appear in different forms, but

---

[18] The general theme of the second part of the poem is the theme of battle itself and the struggle of heroes against overwhelming odds which is such a strong, traditional force in Germanic heroic poetry. A new theme has been added in *Roland*, though, and herein lies the stature of the poem. This theme is the conflict between the concept of the heroic, but doomed fight against odds, as opposed to the immediate appeal for help which would reduce the heroic fight to a delaying action. On which side of the problem would the honor of *dulce France* best be served? The mere fact that such a problem is posed indicates that the *Chanson de Roland* stems from a transitional age where the traditional formulas were becoming inadequate for the broadening conceptions of the poet.

because they are basically the same, they give an *unité du sujet*. Just as the formula expresses a general thought or part of a thought which may be common to different situations, the theme is raised to a high level of generality so as to be applicable to different parts of the poem. And because the poem depends for its unity on the similarity of a general theme viewed in different aspects, the relation of the parts of the poem to each other is paratactic rather than closely co-ordinate. The *jongleur* does, however, provide a peripatetic kind of co-ordination by means of the movements of Charlemagne whose return to Roncevaux connects the second part to the third part, as the third is vaguely connected to the fourth by the march back to Aix.

So far we have been concerned with the generalizing characteristics of the main theme of the poem. It has been seen that these characteristics keep the various parts of the poem concerned with the universal problems of Christian against pagan, French against Saracen, heroes against overwhelming odds, loyalty against treachery, rather than with the special problems of the individual in his particular environment. It was suggested at the beginning of this section that the epic dealt with the general rather than the individual because of the traditional formulas which were used in its composition. A logical extension of this theory would be that the themes which have been discussed above were also traditional so that the poet could assume from the first *laisse* that the Saracens were treacherous because this was the customary belief prevalent in the society,[19] and that the same would be true for the other themes. In fact, a comparison of the *Chanson de Roland* with other *chansons de geste* would confirm this theory. But it is necessary to do more than prove the traditional character of the themes since literary traditions certainly have conventional themes. It should rather be shown that the expression of these themes is traditional in the same way that the formula is traditional, and that the component parts of the themes are always placed on the scene in the same way and in the same order. If this proves true, then there would be a strong basis for

---

[19] Cf. the first two speeches of Blancandrin where his arguments are predicated by the poet on the "Christian" viewpoint that pagans (Saracens) are treacherous.

assuming oral, traditional composition; for a writer would certainly attempt to vary an already parallel structure as much as possible.[20]

To demonstrate these formulaic units, I have chosen the councils in which the leaders meet with their vassals to decide what course of action should be followed. These formulaic groups may be called essential themes because they contribute to the advancement of the story. Of importance also in this respect are the descriptions of heroes and the settings of the battles. These last two themes do not advance the narrative, but give a greater depth to the action. They may be called ornamental themes.

Battle scenes occupy the greater part of the epic and are responsible for the resolution of the plot at Roncevaux, before Saragossa, and in the trial-by-combat at Aix. But the poet needed some means of initiating action. This the tradition provided in the form of the council. On five different occasions in *Roland* councils are convened by the different kings to decide upon a course of action which will then be the subject of that part of the poem. In all cases the same elements are found and frequently the same formulas are used. The logical place to seek the first such council, then, is at the beginning of the poem, the zero point where action certainly must be initiated. In fact, *laisse II* (the first *laisse* is introductory) describes the beginning of such a council:

> Li reis Marsilie esteit en Sarraguce.
> Alez en est en un verger suz l'umbre;
> Sur un perrun de marbre bloi se culchet,
> Envirun lui plus de vint milie humes.
> Il en apelet e ses dux e ses cuntes:
> 'Oez, seignurs, quel pecchet nus encumbret:
> ... ...
> Cunseilez mei cume mi savie hume,
> Si m(e) guarisez e de mort e de hunte.'

One can observe very deliberate steps in this description which may be summarized as, (1) movement of king to council place in the

---

[20] Indeed, Chrétien de Troyes, Marie de France, or Béroul invariably try to show how the combats in their works reflect some particular attribute of the hero. Chrétien always tries to align the fight with the particular quest which is the subject of the *roman*.

open under a tree (orchard, here); (2) mention of the king's seat (here a marble block); (3) enumeration of the king's vassals; (4) official summons of his men (*Il en apelet*, etc., probably some law formula as they are already present); (5) direct address to them and explanation of the matter to be discussed; (6) appeal to vassals for advice on the subject in hand. Following this formal beginning, there will usually be one or two vassals who offer advice. If there is a deadlock, a third party will intervene on behalf of one party or the other and this will then be the final decision. The close of the council will generally be indicated by the king's ordering the execution of the plan decided upon. One sees in this first council which continues through *laisse* VI, that the forces for the first half of the poem have been set in motion and need only the Ganelon-Roland clash (which occurs as a result of the second council, itself a result of the first council) to be complete. If we find that the succeeding councils contain the same elements as the first, in the same order, then it may be safe to assert that the council, as an essential theme, is indeed a traditional theme expressed traditionally.

Laisses XI-XX describe the second council which places the French heroes on the stage for the first time, and illustrates the Ganelon-Roland feud. In effect, by the end of *laisse* XX at line 295, all of the themes which dominate the epic (except the Roland-Oliver episode to be discussed later) will be revealed, and, in a sense, there will remain but the execution. As shall be seen, however, it is in the carrying out of the themes that the genius of the oral poet lies. But to return to the council:

XI

... ...
Li empereres est par matin levet;
Messe e matines ad li reis escultet.
Desuz un pin en est li reis alez,
Ses baruns mandet pur sun cunseill finer:
... ...

XII

Li emper[er]es s'en vait desuz un pin.
Ses baruns mandet pur sun cunseill fenir:
[9 line list of the barons of France follows.]

XIII

'Seignurs barons', dist li emperere Carles
'Li reis Marsilie m'ad tramis ses messages:
... ...
Mais jo ne sai quels en est sis curages.'

It is quite evident that, although considerably expanded, the formal introduction of this second council follows all the steps of the first council with the exception of the second which described Marsile's seat. For the "seat-description" which appears in the introduction to the councils of the pagan kings, Marsile and Baligant, the Christian formula, *messe e matines...*, is substituted in the introduction to Charlemagne's councils. The third step, the enumeration of the vassals, was fulfilled (numerically) in one line of the first introduction, while here it occupies almost all of *laisse* XII. The reason for such an expansion seems to have a formulaic basis, for quite frequently the French barons are enumerated by name, as, for instance, in *laisses* VIII, XII, LIV, CLXII (interesting here because those named are all dead, yet the formulas are the same as before because they do not contain any particularity which would be altered by death), CCXVII-CCXXV. An interesting point in the list under consideration (*laisse* XII) is that Roland, Oliver, and Ganelon are the last three barons named, and Ganelon, in a B-verse epithet, is identified as having committed (past definite) the treason. The same epithet will be applied in the formal introduction to the last council (his trial). The use of the past tense at this early point, when he has just been introduced, is an indication of how little importance questions of time have in the *chansons de geste*. With the conclusion of the formal introduction, Charlemagne takes the sixth step and asks his vassals to advise him. In the three following *laisses,* three different speakers are heard. The words of each are prefaced by the directive, *Il dist al rei* and in two cases the B-verse contains the formula *'Ja mar crerez...* which indicates the disagreement of the speaker with what has been said before. These first speakers are Roland and Ganelon who are deadlocked at the end of the second speech. In the third *laise* (XVI), Naimon intervenes on the side of Ganelon. That his intervention will resolve the deadlock is indicated formulaically by the different B-verse following the usual introduction (different from '*Ja mar crerez...* above):

> E dist al rei: 'Ben l'avez entendud (1. 232)

where it is Ganelon that Naimon thinks we have heard profitably. With the deadlock broken in favor of accepting Marsile's truce, the question of a messenger to confirm the terms arises. Again Charlemagne appeals to his vassals, and does so in the first two lines of three successive *laisses* using the same, or slightly varied formulas. It is in this part of the council that the bitter feud between Roland and Ganelon flares. Ganelon finally leaves the council to go to Saragossa while the rest of the French await his return.

The return of Ganelon from Saragossa is the occasion for the third council. Here the immediate cause is slightly altered since Charlemagne assembles his men to hear Ganelon's report, rather than to settle a problem. But a problem does arise later when a leader of the rearguard must be chosen. Yet see how closely the introduction of this third council follows the introduction of the second council (to the point where the first two lines are the same):

LIV

Li empereres est par matin levet;
Messe e matines ad li reis escultet.
Sur l'erbe verte estut devant sun tref.
[enumeration of barons present]
... ...
E dist al rei: 'Salvez seiez de Deu!

Certainly the last line quoted is not the direct appeal of the king to his vassals which would be the fifth step, for the occasion of the council is different from the usual situation. Nevertheless, Ganelon's greeting is parallel to the fifth step, coming as it does where the king's address would ordinarily fall, and indicates the ease with which the themes may be adjusted to suit different occasions. Parenthetically, it is interesting to note that the B-verse of he last line is a formula of greeting that even the pagan Blancandrin is found using in line 123.

Earlier in his section we noted that from the point of view of general theme, there is little difference between the four parts of the poem. The council of Baligant in *laisse* CXCII further asserts the unity of the poem, at least on the level of formulas and themes. Until this point in the epic, Charlemagne has had only to deal with Marsile. Now, however, the most powerful Saracen emperor answers Marsile's plea and arrives in Spain to fight Charlemagne. This *laisse* begins what has been called the "Baligant" episode by those who disbelieve in the unity of the *Chanson de Roland* in its present form. At any rate, it is the starting point for Baligant's entrance into the story. Naturally enough from the traditional point of view, he must first hold a council so that he and some of his more prominent vassals may be revealed to the listener. The excuse for this essentially dramatic device is the necessity of forming their plans. We already know, however, from the two preceding *laisses* that Baligant has come to fight Charlemagne. Even so, the council is held so that Baligant can be "officially" introduced into the story. The introduction of this council is quite evidently composed of the same formulaic idea as the preceding council-introductions:

CXCII

Clers est li jurz e li soleilz luisant.
Li amiralz est issut del calan:
Espaneliz fors le vait adestrant,
.XVII. reis apres le vunt siwant;
Cuntes e dux i ad ben ne sai quanz.
Suz un lorer, ki est en mi un camp,
Sur l'erbe verte getent un palie blanc:
U[n] faldestoed i unt mis d'olifan;
Desur s'asiet li paien Baligant;
....
'Oiez ore, franc chevaler vaillant!
....

All of the steps outlined above for the formal introduction to councils are fulfilled with the exception of the fourth, the official summons of his men. The sixth step, usually an appeal to the vassals for advice, here takes the form of an oath which he swears before them, and thus, in effect, he is calling on them to be witnesses. As in the other councils, action is initiated which has a direct causal relation to the following part of the story. In this case, Baligant chooses messengers to tell Marsile of his arrival with the result that Marsile offers him Spain if he can conquer Charlemagne.

The final council, held immediately following Charlemagne's return to Aix-la-Chapelle, sets in motion the judgment of Ganelon. Although it is actually a trial, and not a council of state as the others have been, it follows the same lines as the council-patterns already discussed, and is certainly an appeal by Charles to his barons for aid in his suit.[21] Whereas Charles does not participate in his other two councils beyond the formal introduction, he is an active participant here since he has to present his charge of treason, or broken fealty by one of his vassals. Ganelon contends that he did not break fealty with Charlemagne because his feud was a private argument between himself and Roland with whom he had previously severed the *comitatus* bond (*laisse* XXI). Thus the trial is deadlocked as in the first council when Roland and Ganelon were at odds. Again the intervention of a third party, this time the barons that Charles has asked to give judgment; they support Ganelon. Legally Charlemagne has no further recourse with which to resolve the issue, but Thierry of Anjou comes forward to challenge Ganelon to a trial-by-combat. In this combat, Ganelon is defeated and, once again, the council has proved to be the point of departure for the narrative action. Notice that each part of the epic is resolved by combat: Roncevaux, Baligant, and the judgment of Ganelon. And thus, in

---

[21] The formal introduction follows the ones already discussed in five steps: movement of the king to the council place; official summons of his men; direct address and explanation of the problem; appeal to the vassals for assistance.

CCLXXI

Il est escrit en l'anciene geste
Que Carles mandet humes de plusurs teres.
Asemblez sunt ad Ais, a la capele.
Halz est li jurz, mult par est grande la feste,
Dient Alquanz del baron seint Silvestre.
Des ore cumencet le plait e les noveles
De Guenelun, ki traisun ad faite.
Li emperere devant sei l'ad fait traire. AOI.

CCLXXII

'Seignors barons', dist Carlemagnes li reis,
'De Guenelun car me jugez le dreit!
Il fut en l'ost tresque...

true epic fashion, we have the speaking of words and the doing of deeds as the beginning and the end of the narrative.

From the preceding discussion, we have seen that the five councils in the *Chanson de Roland* appear in the same positions each time, i.e. the beginning of an important part of the epic;[22] that the subsequent narrative action stems from the decisions taken in the councils; and that the same steps in the presentation of the council are followed each time, in the same order. Under such circumstances, it does not seem to be an excessive claim to assert that the council is an essential theme in the *Chanson de Roland*, and that it is traditional and formulaic.

There is another frequently recurring formulaic group which must be called ornamental, as it does not contribute to the action of the story. Nevertheless, the artistic contribution of this group, the phrases descriptive of the general appearance of the heroes, is considerable. Since this theme is non-essential to the narrative action, it does not have to be used by the *jongleur* in any specific order or place, but can be inserted at his will using unnecessary enjambement. Similarly, the amplitude of the descriptive material varies from one or two lines during a combat, to a whole *laisse*, on two occasions where the leader of one side or the other is being "described". One must use the word 'described', but in actual fact, the formulas do not describe Roland or Baligant as individuals, for they might be applied to any warrior of heroic stature. In practice, one distinguishes those warriors who are more heroic by the number of combats they are allotted, and by the number of descriptive phrases devoted to them. Such formulaic groups are usually found preceding a battle or one of the heroes' combats in a battle, but they also occur (without the reference to weapons) in other than battle contexts, as for instance, the six-line description of Ganelon (11. 28-285) in Charlemagne's first council. Attention may be called to Appendix III where some important examples of this type of ornamental theme are cited. Their similarity to each other and to the several examples quoted from other *chansons de geste* again offers telling evidence of the traditional nature of the themes in the *Chanson de Roland*.

---

[22] There are two councils at the beginning of the poem: one to initiate pagan action and one, the direct result of the first, to initiate Christian action.

At the beginning of the discussion of the structure of the poem, we noted (note 18) that in the Roncevaux episode, the *jongleur* had posed a conflict which he did not really have the means to express fully.[23] For the conflict —whether to fight or summon aid— is really a psychological one which only Roland as captain of the rearguard, can decide. As presented in *laisses* LXXXIII-LXXXVIII, it seems to be a dialogue between Roland and Oliver in which each represents an opposing view, much as we have seen on two different occasions in the councils. But here there is no third party intervention to resolve the issue, and it is Roland himself in *laisses* CXXVII-CXXIX who proposes the plan which he had previously opposed. He has obviously changed his mind, which implies a psychological process, although the external events have some bearing on his decision. But nowhere does the poet mention Roland as "thinking" about this problem. Furthermore, Roland, on the second occasion, uses combinations of the same formulas Oliver had used when he first urged Roland to sound his horn. The implications of the conflict within Roland underlie the whole Roncevaux episode and influence the action of the next part. It is clear, then, that the problem has a dramatic importance much greater than its explicit presentation would indicate. If such is the case, the *jongleur* has succeeded in surpassing the restrictions of the formulaic speech, and an analysis of this achievement will reveal that the profundity of his vision goes beyond the stage which Notopoulos, in the above quotation, called "formulaic thinking". This achievement will then be a basis for evaluation. But such a basis can only be established by an analysis of a work within its convention. Once this analysis has been made, it will then be possible to show how a work differs from others like it, and whether the difference makes it a higher achievement or an inferior imitation.

The suggestion to call for reinforcements is made by Oliver after he has been the first to comprehend the vastness of the approaching Saracen forces. The suggestion seems reasonably well-founded on the realistic proposition: they are many and we are few, *ergo* let us call on Charlemagne's force. Roland replies with the quite natural

---

[23] For the method followed in the fourth part of my paper, I am indebted to Adam Parry's article, "The Language of Achilles", *TAPA*, 87 (1956), pp. 1-7.

concern that he will lose his heroic reputation in France if he seeks help. Reassuringly, he reminds Oliver of the effectiveness of his sword and avows that they can match the Saracens. These are the basic positions of Oliver and Roland, the one founded evidently on a realistic appraisal of the relative size of the two opposing forces, and the other based on the heroic over-estimation that the "twelve peers" are a match for the overwhelming pagan force. Neither position is a complicated one in appearance, and yet each represents a way of thinking which reaches deep into their personalities. One certainly would not feel this depth, however, if the *jongleur* let the question pass after the first *laisse*. But he does not. In the next *laisse* Oliver restates his proposal, this time using the verb *sucurre* which indicates his feeling that they are not just in need of light reinforcement, but real aid, as though they were helpless. As Oliver's request becomes more urgent, Roland gives more social reasons for his refusal to sound the horn. In the first *laisse*, he cited his heroic reputation (*los*); here he speaks of his obligation to his family and to *France dulce* for whose sakes he should show no cowardice. It becomes apparent that this problem has wide implications, and that the rearguard is not just a part of Charlemagne's army, but now represents France against the Saracens. They are heroes and should conduct themselves accordingly, as Roland's reference each time to his sword and the damage it will wreak reminds us. When Oliver, in *laisse* LXXXV, urges for the third time that Roland recall Charles, the importance of the conflict is emphasized beyond any single aspect of the poem to this point, since this is the first time that three consecutive *laisses* have been devoted to the same subject. Their similar wording, thrice repeated in the same order, forces our attention to focus on this problem. But again in this third *laisse* there is only the basic statement of difference: Oliver is worried about the fate of the rearguard, while Roland is concerned with their honor. Although the order of events in the fourth *laisse* of the sequence, is the same as the preceding three, i.e. Oliver speaks first, then Roland responds, the speeches are not parallel, since each of the men expresses another aspect of the situation. Oliver does not mention the horn nor Charlemagne, but rather elaborates his statement in the first *laisse* of the series: the multitude of the approaching Saracens and the inadequacy of their own numbers. The ratio of lines devoted to each of these two forces in the *laisse* is three to one, so that the larger pagan force has a greater number of lines concerned with it than does the smaller French force. So Oliver's viewpoint throughout these four *laisses* has remained static, always centered on the realistic comparison of numbrs. Roland, on the other hand, has cited three reasons —personal honor, family honor, national honor— why they should not summon aid. The variety of his answers, as compared with the sameness of Oliver's urging, indicates that Roland is engaged in some mental process, even if it is only to defend his natural impulse to fight. That discretion is the better part of valor has never been an heroic attribute, at least in heroic poetry. In this fourth *laisse*, as in the other three, Roland cites two more reasons for fighting. The first is that it would not be pleasing to God if Roland sullied the *valur* of France by yielding before the pagans. Here again we find a *reprise* of one of the main themes: that the French are the people of God, and as such, the defenders of the faith. To Roland such a retreat from the heroic ideal (based on faith as well as tradition as we see from Charlemagne's combat with Baligant) would be a manifest lack of faith displeasing to God. Second, they are called the "twelve peers", for which they are esteemed beyond all the fighting men of France: they are above ordinary men as we understand by the word "heroic" in the Homeric sense, or rather in the Old Testament sense since Christianity precludes their being related to the gods. Charlemagne esteems them because of their fighting prowess, so they must live up to that ideal or die:

> Melz voeill murir que huntages me venget.   (1. 1091

Oliver may have a more realistic view of the situation, but Roland understands far better their *raison d'être,* although the limits of formulaic diction make it difficult for this almost metaphysical idea to be expressed.[24]

---

[24] Apropos of the necessarily restrained expression of this central psychological conflict, it is interesting to note that Jean Frappier finds even the equine vocabulary extremely economical in comparison with later *chansons de geste*:

> Il saute d'abord aux yeux que la *Chanson de Roland* n'utilise qu'un jeu restreint d'épithètes. Elle emploie seulement *bon* et *courant*, qui restent d'ailleurs les adjectifs fondamentaux du voca-

At this point (*laisse* LXXXVII), before the fifth and final attempt by Oliver to have Charles recalled, the *jongleur* intervenes with descriptive epithets which, again, touch upon the general qualities of the heroes, but not upon the individual personalities that cause their heroic actions. He indicates that both Oliver and Roland are right, and that each is moved by high ideals, but in the end we see that Roland's view is the more profound in the perspective of their purpose and time. To Oliver's fifth restatement of the necessity to recall the main army, Roland firmly replies that they will stand and fight to show that they are not cowards. His final word on the subject fills the next *laisse*, where he places their obligation to fight in a feudal context, saying in effect that the king has given him his sword, and that to acquit oneself as a *nobilie vassal* it is sometimes necessary to suffer greatly. The *laisse*, and thus the whole series end with the words *nobilie vassal* which seem to contain the crux of the medieval hero's existence since he was not only the vassal of the emperor, but also, through the emperor, of God. This position is verified in the following *laisse* where Archbishop Turpin, next to Roland and Oliver the most effective fighter of the French heroes, blesses the French force and assures them that they are fighting for God, who will not deny his warriors Paradise (which still seems suspiciously close to Valhalla).

After this dramatic prelude which certainly increases the importance of the impending battle, the advance guard of the Saracens attacks. The order of the battle is very important to the second "horn" episode because of its relation to the interpretation of Roland's final decision to summon Charlemagne. Does his later decision to sound the Olifant indicate a basic change in his position, a conversion to Oliver's original point of view? Roland was at first confident that they would be able to defeat the Saracens. Actually, the French do defeat the advance guard of the pagans which contains the "twelve peers" of the Saracen army, including Marsile's son.

---

bulaire hippique ... elle ne connaît que trois épithètes de couleur (sor, brun, blanc), elle ignore toute épithète géographique pour les destriers. On ne peut qu'être frappé par cette discrétion, cette économie des moyens.

La Technique littéraire des chansons de geste, Actes du Colloque de Liège (septembre 1957), (Paris, 1959), p. 98.

With the arrival of the main body of the Saracens, however, the French are clearly doomed to succumb to the sheer weight of numbers of the enemy. Nevertheless, the French wreak great havoc among the enemy, which is forced to appeal for more aid (*laisse* CXXVI). With only sixty of the French remaining, Roland is forcibly reminded that the finest of the French chevaliers are lying dead on the field. At this point, the very ends which he felt he was serving when he refused to summon Charles seem to be defeated:

> 'Bel sire, chers cumpainz, pur Deu, que vos enhaitet?
> Tanz bons vassals veez gesir par tere!
> Pleindre poums France dulce, la bele:
> De tels baróns cum or remeint deserte!
> E! reis, amis, que vos ici nen estes?
> (ll. 1693-97).

If Roland's reasons for not recalling Charles were based on the social concern for the honor of France, family, liege lord, and God, it is clear that this reconsideration of his former position has equally a social (as opposed to personal) basis. His lament is directed toward the loss to France of the dead barons. In other words, the tangible evidence of so many dead barons seems a contradiction to the heroic ideals which he expressed before the fight. That they died honorably, and therefore did realize those heroic ideals is the type of leisurely abstract reasoning which ill fits the battle-field. For although the heroic ideals which he first expressed were abstract, they were based on the real fact that the French rearguard was composed of superior warriors who lived by and even for fighting. Now that they are dead, it seems that they have been defeated. Here, then, is the basic conflict within Roland: the result of the battle appears to contradict the reasons for which it was undertaken. These ideals permitted Roland to predict three times before the battle:

> Jo vos plevis, tuz sont jugez a mort.
> (ll. 1058, 1069, 1080).

Roland was referring to the Saracens, but ironically his prediction is proving true for his own force. It is impossible to tell exactly what is Roland's mental reaction to this apparent contradiction, for we can see only his actions, but evidently the shock of the reversal has caused him to realize that he may have been wrong in not recalling Charles. Personally, he remains the heroic figure to the end: fighting and dying well. But as leader of the rearguard, it is evident that he becomes uncertain of his duty. Line 1697 seems almost a plea for Charles' guidance as well as his material assistance, and this feeling is reinforced in the line following when he turns to Oliver for advice. Notice also that in the next two *laisses* the order of the first series (*laisses* LXXXIII-LXXXVII) is reversed with Roland here proposing to sound the horn, while Oliver argues against the proposition. It is not the deadlock which here interests us (that is resolved as in the councils by the intervention of a third party, Turpin), but the reorientation of Roland's viewpoint. The only way we can really recognize the significant conflict within Roland is by considering the importance of the first episode, by following the progress of the battle, and then by analyzing, as we have done, his words in *laisse* CXXVIII in relation to the difference in the reality of the scene around him and that which he predicted. Then the simple statement, *Cornerai L'olifant* (devoid in itself of emotion), coming as it does after all that has gone before, reflects an emotional perspective in which Roland is the central figure (since the struggle is central to him), but which is also shared by the listener who has seen the growing disparity between the heroic prediction and the actual event.

Such an experience is neither traditional nor formulaic since the poet has inadequate means to give it full expression. It is clearly the work of an individual creativity which could, by deliberate repetition of important parts and by careful arrangement of the order of events, transcend the limitations of speech to hint at a complex reaction, a subtle character development taking place within the protagonist, Roland. If the work can be shown to have made such an optimum use of its convention that it has, in effect, succeeded in rising above the limitations of that convention, then this should be one basis for its evaluation as a superior artistic creation. Many critics have acclaimed the *Chanson de Roland* as a superior artistic achievement, but none has based his claim on the optimum use and ultimate surpassing of the limitations of traditional diction. And yet all of the aspects of the poem which have been considered in this paper indicate that the text certainly is the result of oral rather than literary diction. In the last analysis, it makes no difference whether the poem were given its final arrangement by the man responsible for the manuscript. It is the text which offers itself to criticism, and this criticism can only be achieved completely if one is fully aware of the convention in which it was formed: oral, formulaic, and traditional diction.

APPENDIX I

Formulaic Schemes

Analysis: Tetrasyllabic Hemistich (A-verse) in first 2000 lines.

I. *E plus three syllable* name, pronoun or noun.*
   Purpose: to fit a name into the A-verse; the *E*, while having an expletive and/or conjunctive force, neither alters nor modifies the name.

   Examples:

       E Berenger   (11. 1304, 1624)
       E Priamun   (1. 65)   55 uses of this type
       E Oliver   (10 times)
       E l'arcevesque   (4 times)
       E li Franceis   (3 times)
       E vers Franceis   (1. 1163; cf. 1. 1162: *vers sarrazins*. Here the 3-syllable noun obviates the need for the filler, *E*.)
       E la cervele   (1. 1356)
       E sis cumpainz   (3 times)

A. *E/En plus place name and adjective* (the latter only when place name is one syllable). The Adjective provides necessary two syllables when place name is only one syllable.

   Examples:

       En Rencesvals   (7 times)
       E! France dulce   (1. 1985)   49 uses of this type
       En dulce France   (8 times)
       En Sarraguce   (6 times)

   This type of formula is used also in the hexasyllabic hemistich (B-verse), where a verb is usually added to fill out the extra two syllables.

---

* Since the hypersyllable, so frequent in *Roland*, is not counted, I include nouns or titles which may actually be four syllables.

Examples:
    ad estet en Espaigne   (1. 2)
    sunt remes en Espaigne   (1. 826)
    esteit en Sarraguce   (1. 10)

II. *Name/noun plus être.*
Purpose: to prepare a B-verse which asserts some quality or state of the A-verse.

Examples:

La bataille est	(5 times)	
Margariz est	(1. 1311)	
Fust chrestiens	(1. 899)	28 uses of this type
Sarrazins est	(1, 932)	
Li destrers est	(1. 1490)	

III. *Two names/nouns in A-verse.*
Purpose: usually used in catalogues or to permit B-verse to apply to two people, groups, or things.

Examples:

Francs e paiens	(1. 1187)	
Franc e paien	(1. 1397)	
Pluie e gresilz	(1. 1425)	9 uses of this type
D'osbercs e de helmes	(1. 1789)	
Osbercs e helmes	(1. 1809)	

There is a more prevalent use (34 times) of this formulaic type in the B-verse, however, where it is used in conjunction with such A-verse formulas as *Ensembl' od lui.*

Examples:
    Oliver e Rollant   (11. 947, 1413, 1512)
    Rollant e Oliver   (11. 104, 1680)
    e Gerin e Gerers   (11. 107, 174)
    Guenes e Blancandrins   (11. 402, 413)
    e la bronie e le cors   (1. 1586)

IV. *Title/name/noun plus descriptive adjective.* (The latter in cases where name is only two or three syllables.)
Purpose: to modify name in some descriptive fashion. Thus by this system, the jongleur can give in the A-verse some indication of rank or quality to person or noun which is subject or object (in case of inversion) of B-verse.

Examples:
    Li quens Rollant   (20 times)
    Li emper[er]es   (24 times)
    Li reis Marsilie   (14 times)

APPENDIX 45

    Li arcesvesques   (7 times)
    Seignurs barons   (12 times)
    Li duze per   (13 times)
    Li bons osbercs   (7 times)
    le blanc osberc   (11. 1329, 1946)   278 uses of this type
    De sun osberc   (4 times)
    Ma { bone { espee }
    Sun { bon { espiet }   (9 times)
    Tere major   (5 times)
    La bone sele   (11. 1373, 1588)

A. In certain cases where both A- and B-verses will contain descriptive remarks, the verb *être* may be used.

   Examples:
    Halt sunt li pui   (3 times)
    Li reis est fiers   (1. 56)
    Rollant est proz   (1. 1093)
    Franceis sunt morz   (1. 1726)
    Franceis sunt bon   (1. 1080)

V. *Collective noun plus verb.*
   Purposè: to introduce B-verse descriptive of action of either the *laisse* or the A-verse.

   Examples:
    Franceis de[s]cendent   (11. 1136, 1797)
    Franceis murrunt   (6 times)   51 uses of this type
    Dient Franceis   (12 times)
    Dient paien   (5 times)
    Paien escrient   (1. 1906; Jenkins 1. 46a - supplied from V^7 C.)
    Paien chevalchent   (1. 710)

VI. *Discourse Introduction.*
   Purpose: to introduce discourse which will begin in B-verse and may continue for several or more lines.

A. *Dist plus name or indirect object.*

   Examples:
    Dist Blancandrins   (6 times)
    E dist al { rei }
            { cunte }   (15 times)
    Dist al paien   (11. 1608, 1632, 1898)
    Dist li paiens   (1. 537)
    Dist l'arcevesque   (4 times)
    Dist Oliver   (12 times)   131 uses of this type
    Dist li Sarrazins   (1. 550)
    Ço dist Rollant   (10 times)
    Ço dist li reis   (9 times)

>
> Ço dist li quens   (ll. 787, 1935)
> Ço dist Marsilies   (5 times)

B. *Respunt plus name.*

Examples:

> Respunt Marsilies   (l. 424)
> Ço respunt Guenes   (l. 358)
> Respunt Rollant   (12 times)
> Guenes respunt   (16 times)

VII. *Noun plus verb.* (This would also include what has already been demonstrated as "discourse introduction". Because of the latter's special function, it is given a separate heading.)
Purpose: to permit a noun, title, or name to move or act in the A-verse in a manner which the B-verse will make explicit as follows:

> Carles comandet que face sun servise   (l. 298)

Sometimes the B-verse will be filled by an epithet or descriptive phrase or clause which modifies the A-verse, as:

> Guenes i vint, ki la traïsun fist   (l. 178)

or:

> Guenes i vint, li fels, li parjurez.   (l. 674)

But mostly, this formulaic system is used to describe action and movement of characters.

Examples:

> Si { vunt / vait } ferir   (10 times)
> Vait le ferir   (5 times)
> Sun { / le } cheval broche(t)   (11 times)
> Siet el cheval   (6 times)
> Tient Durendal   (ll. 1339, 1583, 1870)
> Trait Durendal   (l. 1324)   349 uses of this type
> Tient Halteclere   (ll. 1550, 1953)
> Oliver sent   (ll. 1952, 1965, 2010)
> Marsilie vient   (l. 1449)
> Marsilie veit   (l. 1467)
> Vint i { Gerins / Otes / Gerart / etc. }   (5 times)
> Marsilies mandet   (l. 848)

APPENDIX

VIII. *Adjective/adverb/preposition plus noun/verb.*
Purpose: most frequently used to indicate position (*par, devant, parmi, desuz, sur*); quantity (*mult, tanz, tro*); possession (*sa*).

Examples:

Desuz un pin   (11. 114, 165)
Unc mais nuls hom   (1. 1040)
Unches mais hom   (1. 1461)
Unches nuls hom   (1. 1477)
Unches n'amai   (1. 1486)
Unc nel sunast   (1. 1769)
Mult grant { eschec / venjance / damage }   (11. 99, 1459, 1885)
Devant Marsilie   (5 times)
Devant Rollant   (1. 1875)   186 uses of this type
Tanz riches reis   (11. 527, 542, 555)
Tant bon Franceis   (1. 1401)
Tanz bons vassals   (1. 1494)
Par tantes teres   (11. 525, 540, 553)
Sa rereguarde   (9 times)
Pleine sa hanste   (6 times)
Set cenz cameilz   (4 times)
Par } .XX. hostages   (11. 572, 646, 679)
 E }
.XX. milie { Francs / ad escuz }   (4 times)

IX. There are besides various whole-line formulaic expressions, such as the following expressions of vassalage or greeting:

Serez ses hom par honur e par ben.   (1. 39)
[S]erai ses hom par amur e par feid   (1. 86)
[cf. also: Tes hom serai par amur e par feid   (1. 3893)]
Tu n'ies mes hom ne jo ne sui tis sire.   (1. 297)
Sil saluerent par amur e par bien   (1. 121)
                                4 uses of this type

X. Certain whole-line formulaic expressions which have a proverbial character are also to be found:

Paien unt tort e chrestiens unt dreit   (1. 1015)
Melz voeill murir que huntage me venget.   (1. 1091)
Mielz voeill murir que hunte nus seit retraite   (1. 1701)
Tort nos ad fait: nen est dreiz qu'il s'en lot.   (1. 1950)
                                4 uses of this type

XI. There are, in addition, certain whole-line fromulas associated with Charlemagne:

> Li empereres en tint sun chef enclin (1, 139).
> Li emper[er]e en tint sun chef enbrunc (11. 214, 771).
> Ses baruns mandet pur sun cunseill { (finer) } (11. 166, 169).
> { (fenir) }

XII. A formula permitting a liaison between a speech in preceding line(s) and an action in B-verse or in following lines may also be seen:

> A icez moz   (7 times).
> Iço vus mandet   (11. 124, 430)   11 uses of this type
> Quar ço vos mandet   (1. 470).
> E si vos mandet   (1. 680).

TOTAL: 1157 formulaic expressions in the tetrasyllabic hemistiches of the first 2000 lines of the *Chanson de Roland*.

APPENDIX II

Types of Enjambement

A. Lines 1-500 of the *Chanson de Roland*.

1. Unnecessary Enjambement.

laisse I	11.	1-2, 5-6, 7-8.
II		16-17, 18-19, 20-21, 22-23.
III		30-31-32-33, 38-39, 40-41, 44-45-46.
IV		47-48, 58-59-60.
V		64-68, 72-73, 75-76.
VI		81-82, 83-86.
VII		89-90.
VIII		97-98, 99-100, 101-02, 104-07, 112-13, 114-15, 117-18.
IX		123-24, 125-26, 127-31, 132-33.
X		145-46, 147-48, 149-50, 151-53.
XI		—
XII		170-76.
XIII		182-86.
XIV		194-95.
XV		220-21, 224-27.
XVI		231-33, 236-38.
XVII		244-45, 249-50.
XVIII		252-53, 261-62.
XIX		—
XX		274-76, 281-82, 283-84, 289-91.
XXI		300-01.
XXII		—
XXIII		312-14.
XXIV		319-20, 323-24, 325-26.
XXV		—
XXVI		—
XXVII		343-44, 349-50, 353-54, 355-56, 361-64.
XXVIII		366-67, 370-71, 372-73.
XXIX		378-80, 381-82, 384-85, 387-88, 389-90.
XXX		392-94, 398-99.
XXXI		402-04, 405-06, 407-08, 411-12.
XXXII		416-17, 421-22.
XXXIII		426-27, 428-29, 430-31, 432-34, 435-36.

APPENDIX

XXXIV 447-49.
XXXV 451-52, 453-54, 457-61, 462-63.
XXXVI 470-71, 475-76, 479-80.
XXXVII 488-91, 492-93, 495-96.

231 uses.

2. No Enjambement.

laisse I	11. 3, 4, 9.
II	10-15.
III	24-29, 34-37, 42, 43.
IV	49, 50, 53-57, 61.
V	62, 63, 69-71, 74, 77.
VI	78-80, 87, 88.
VII	91-95.
VIII	96, 103, 108-111, 116, 119-21.
IX	122, 134-138.
X	139-144, 154-56.
XI	157-167.
XII	168, 169, 177-79.
XIII	180, 181, 187-92.
XIV	193, 196-98, 201, 204-06, 209-13.
XV	214-19, 228, 229.
XVI	230, 235, 241-43.
XVII	246-48, 251.
XVIII	254-60, 263.
XIX	264, 273.
XX	277-80, 285-88, 293-95.
XXI	296-99, 302.
XXII	305-09.
XXIII	310, 311. 315-18.
XXIV	321, 322, 327-30.
XXV	331-36.
XXVI	337-41.
XXVII	342, 345-48, 351, 352. 357-60, 365.
XXVIII	368, 369. 374-76.
XXIX	377, 383, 386, 391.
XXX	395-97, 400, 401.
XXXI	409, 410, 413.
XXXII	414, 415, 418-20, 423, 424.
XXXIII	425, 437-440.
XXXIV	441-46, 450.
XXXV	455, 456, 464-67.
XXXVI	468, 469, 472-74, 477, 478, 481-84.
XXXVII	485-87, 494, 497-500.

261 uses.

APPENDIX 51

3. Necessary Enjambement.

   laisse IV ll.   51-52.
         XV   222-23.
         XVI   239-40.
         XXII   303-04.

                                                             8 uses.

B. Lines 2933-3034 of the *Chanson de Roland*.

1. Unnecessary Enjambement.

   laisse CCX ll.   2936-37, 2938-42.
         CCXI   2946-47, 2948-49, 2955-57, 2958-59.
         CCXII   —
         CCXIII   2962-65, 2970-71.
         CCXIV   2974-75, 2976-77, 2979-80, 2985-86.
         CCXV   2987-90.
         CCXVI   2999-3003.
         CCXVII   3015-20.
         CCXVIII 3031-32.

                                                             47 uses.

2. No Enjambement

   laisse CCX ll.   2933-35, 2943, 2944.
         CCXI   2949, 2950.
         CCXII   2951-54, 2960-61.
         CCXIII   2966-69, 2972, 2973.
         CCXIV   2978, 2981-84.
         CCXV   2991-98.
         CCXVI   3004, 3005, 3009, 3010, 3013.
         CCXVII   3014, 3025.
         CCXVIII 3026-30.

                                                             44 uses.

3. Necessary Enjambement.

   laisse CCXVI ll. 3006-07, 3011-12.
         CCXVII   3021-22, 23-24.
         CCXVIII   3033-34.

                                                             10 uses.

C. Lines 684-749 of *Le Chevalier de la charrete* (éd. de Mario Roques, CFMA).

APPENDIX

    1. No Enjambement: 684-89, 691, 693, 695, 696, 699, 702, 706, 707, 709, 710, 713, 719, 722, 724, 729, 732, 734, 735, 737, 739, 740, 743, 747, 748.

31 uses.

    2. Necessary Enjambement: 690, 692, 694, 697, 698, 700, 701, 703-05, 708, 711, 712, 714, 720, 721, 723, 725, 726, 728, 731, 733, 736, 738, 741, 742, 744, 746, 749.

30 uses.

    3. Unnecessary Enjambement: 716, 717, 718, 730.

4 uses.

D. Lines 2466-2531 of *Le Chevalier de la Charrete*.

    1. No Enjambement: 2467-69, 2473, 2480, 2483, 2484, 2487-89, 2491, 2492, 2496, 2498, 2499, 2503, 2504, 2507, 2509, 2513, 2515, 2517-19, 2521, 2522, 2526, 2527, 2529, 2531.

30 uses.

    2. Necessary Enjambement: 2466, 2470-72, 2474-79, 2481, 2482, 2485, 2486, 2490, 2493, 2496, 2500-02, 2505, 2506, 2508, 2510, 2514, 2516, 2520, 2523, 2530.

29 uses.

    3. Unnecessary Enjambement: 2494-95, 2511-12, 2524-25.

6 uses.

E. Chanson du roi Thibaut IV de Navarre (XIII^eS.)

    1. No Enjambement: 2, 5, 7, 9, 11, 14, 17, 19, 21, 23, 25, 26, 28, 30, 35, 38.

16 uses.

    2. Necessary Enjambement: 1, 3, 4, 6, 8, 10, 12, 13, 18, 20, 22, 24, 27, 29, 31, 36, 37, 39.

18 uses.

    3. Unnecessary Enjambement: 15-16, 32-33-34, 40-41.

7 uses.

APPENDIX III

Ornamental Themes in the *Chanson de Roland*
and in Several other *Chansons de Geste*

I.
Roland LXXIX

Paien s'adubent des osbercs sarazineis,
Tuit li plusur en sunt (saraguzeis) dublez en treis.
Lacent lor elmes mult bons sarraguzeis,
Ceignent espees de l'acer vianeis;
Escuz unt genz, espiez valentineis,
E gunfanuns blancs e blois e vermeilz.
Laissent les mulz e tuz les palefreiz,
Es destrers muntent, si chevalchent estreiz.
... ...

Roland CXXXVI

... ...
Franceis descendent, si adubent lor cors
D'osbercs e de helmes e d'espees a or.
Escuz unt genz e espiez granz e forz,
E gunfanuns blancs e vermeilz e blois.
Es destrers muntent tuit li barun de l'ost.
... ...

Roland CCXXVIII

... ...
Paien descendent pur lur cors aduber.
Li amiralz ne se voelt demurer:
Vest une bronie dunt li pan sunt sasfret,
Lacet sun elme, ki ad or est gemmet,
Puis ceint s'espee al senestre costet.
... ...

APPENDIX

La Chanson de Guillaume XII

... ...
Dunc li vestent une broine [brónie] malt vele e cler,
E un vert healme li lacent en la teste;
Dunc ceint s'espee, la brant burni vers terre,
E une grant targe tint par manvele;
... ...
E blanche enseigne li lacent tresque a tere.
... ...

Guillaume LXXXVII

Dunc li vestirent une broigne mult bele,
E un vert healme li lacent en la teste.
Willame li ceinst l'espee al costé senestre;
Une grant targe prist par la manvele;

II.   ### *Roland* CXIV

... ...
Li destrers est e curanz e aates,
Piez a copiez e les gambes ad plates,
Curte la quisse e la crupe bien large,
Lungs les costez e l'eschine ad ben halte,
Blance la cue e la crignete jalne,
Petites les oreilles, la teste tute falve;
Beste nen est nule ki encontre lui alge.
... ...

III. ### *Roland* XX

... ...
Vairs out [les oilz] e mult fier lu visage,
Gent out le cors e les costez out larges;
Tant par fut bels tuit si per l'en esguardent.
... ...

Roland LXXII

... ...
Cors ad mult gent e le vis fier e cler;
Puis que il est sur sun cheval muntet,
Mult se fait fiers de ses armes porter;
De vasselage est il ben alosez.
... ...

Roland CCXXVIII

... ...
En sun destrer Baligant est muntet;
... ...
La forcheure ad asez grant li ber,
Graisles as flancs e larges les costez;
Gros ad le piz, belement est mollet,
Lees les espalles e le vis ad mult cler,
Fier le visage, le chef recercelet,
Tant par ert blancs cume flur en estet;
De vasselage est suvent esprovet.
... ...

Floovant LXXII

... ...
Ou destré est montee, qui tot vai l'anblaurë
Molt bien resanblai home a la grant forchaüre.

IV.   ### *Roland* CCXXXVIII

Grant est la plaigne e large la cuntree.
Luisent cil elme as perres d'or gemmees,
E cez escuz e cez bronies safrees,
E cez espiez, cez enseignes fermees.
Sunent cez graisles, les voiz en sunt mult cleres;
De l'olifan haltes sunt les menees.
... ...

Roland LXXXI

... ...
E Sarrazins, ki tant sunt asemblez.
Luisent cil elme, ki ad or sunt gemmez,
E cil escuz e cil osbercs safrez
E cil espiez, cil gunfanun fermez.
... ...

Roland CLXIX

Halt sunt li pui e mult halt les arbres.
Quatre perruns i ad luisant de marbre.
... ...

Roland CXXXVIII

Halt sunt li pui e tenebrus e grant,
Li val parfunt e les ewes curant.
Sunent cil graisle e derere e devant,
E tuit rachatent encuntre l'olifant.
... ...

Roland CXXXVII

Esclargiz est li vespres e li jurz.
Cuntre le soleil reluisent cil adub,
Osbercs e helmes i getent grant flambour,
E cil escuz, ki ben sunt peinz a flurs,
E cil espiez, cil oret gunfanun.
... ...

The Department of Romance Studies Digital Arts and Collaboration Lab at the University of North Carolina at Chapel Hill is proud to support the digitization of the North Carolina Studies in the Romance Languages and Literatures series.

www.ingramcontent.com/pod-product-compliance
Lightning Source LLC
Chambersburg PA
CBHW020422230426
43663CB00007BA/1283